WOMEN'S ISSUES

Kathleen Rowe

HAZELDEN®

First published March, 1986.

Copyright © 1986, Hazelden Foundation.
All rights reserved. No portion of this publication may be reproduced in any manner without the written permission of the publisher.

ISBN: 0-89486-361-4

Printed in the United States of America.

Editor's Note:
Hazelden Educational Materials offers a variety of information on chemical dependency and related areas. Our publications do not necessarily represent Hazelden or its programs, nor do they officially speak for any Twelve Step organization.

CONTENTS

Introduction 1

Powerlessness 2

Success and Failure 6

Self-Image and Self-Esteem 9

Personal Responsibility 13

Guilt 15

Shame 18

Choices 20

Relationships 23

Faith 27

Fulfillment and Self-Actualization 30

INTRODUCTION

Whether it's during a group discussion, a conversation between two people, or in one person's private thoughts, certain topics come up again and again when people examine their lives in the hope of making them better. Since the late 1960s, many women have been questioning the directions their lives have taken, the beliefs they have held, and, most importantly, the meaning or purpose of their lives. Sometimes this questioning is painful, sometimes frightening, certainly confusing. But again and again people find that when they resolve the questions and begin to act on their conclusions, life can hold new hope, excitement, and accomplishment.

The questioning process is crucial for the full recovery of chemically dependent women. Until recently it was difficult, even impossible, for a recovering chemically dependent female to find a group in which she could discuss questions that weighed on her mind; they were distinctly about women's issues — issues unique to women's life experiences. But now, as more discussion groups are formed specifically for recovering women, these topics are examined openly and honestly, and there is new hope that these women can find the courage to lead full, drug-free lives.

The purpose of this booklet is to review some of the major issues that come up in recovering women's group sessions. In particular, it's designed to show how *any* problem or issue can be handled successfully whether you are in a group or, for whatever reason, are dealing with a problem on your own. Topics such as guilt, powerlessness, responsibility, self-actualization; all of these and others are burning issues for women today. Perhaps some of these present special concerns for recovering women who may have tried to deal with them in the past. At that time, the burden of addiction obscured thinking, tangled emotions, and compounded any existing life challenge by distorting reality.

Basically, the approach to any life question or problem, or the setting of a worthy goal can be taken in several steps. These steps are
1) defining the problem/challenge/goal and evaluating its purpose;
2) brainstorming possible solutions;
3) selecting the most viable solution;
4) planning to achieve the goal;
5) implementing the plan.

Nothing in this booklet is to be taken as the definitive answer to a particular problem, topic, or life challenge. You may even disagree with some of the remarks made here, *for each person's answer* must be suited specifically to her life and individuality. But the booklet can serve as a guide, outline, or program for *finding* those answers suited to the individual. In that quest, we wish you well.

POWERLESSNESS

*"We admitted we were powerless over alcohol — that our lives had become unmanageable."**

It is frightening to admit we are powerless over anything — alcohol or other drugs, food, or any other substance. How utterly helpless and vulnerable we feel to say it; it seems like admitting defeat. What can we possibly do? Yet, as frightening as it may seem, this is the first of the Twelve Steps to recovery. These are the words that drive us to seek help. In the long run, these are the words that start us on the road to gaining power and control over our lives.

There are many things in life over which we have little or no power. For example, all of us are truly powerless to stop the rain. Not one of us could stop an earthquake. And we all know death

---

*See p. 35 for the Twelve Steps of Alcoholics Anonymous.

is inevitable; we cannot stop it. While both men and women could easily come up with similar lists of things over which they feel powerless, the issue of powerlessness is a special case for women. Let's face it — whether we're traditionalists, feminists, or somewhere in between, many of us were raised to be helpless. Powerlessness is inaction, stagnation, doing nothing — and we women all grew up hearing an awful lot of "don'ts" and "can'ts."

Think back to your childhood. What did it feel like when you suddenly realized there were many things you couldn't do just because you were a girl? Were you bewildered? Confused? In addition to feeling confused, you probably felt other emotions: frustration, anger, and/or the sadness of defeat. Does it sound familiar? Many of us heard this attitude expressed at home (when we were children and **truly** "powerless"), in school, church, and from society as we grew up. But wait a minute — it sounds like we're giving ourselves a very good excuse for not taking charge of our lives. There certainly are a lot of people to blame for putting us down and holding us there: parents, teachers, ministers, and the man on the street. And if we admit it to ourselves, sometimes it's a cozy and comfortable feeling to curl up inside our powerlessness and blame others for our failure to actively control our lives.

Writing It Down
Take a few minutes right now to make up a list of all the things over which you feel powerless. Don't read on until you've spent at least five minutes thinking about and making up your list.

What does the list look like? Some items might be:
my drinking
my spouse's temper
finances
my children's school work
lack of job opportunities
inability to go to school (for any reason)
getting older
my love life

Depressing, isn't it? We may feel tense and exhausted just thinking about things that are crucially important in our lives but over which we have little control. And what's really discouraging is that some of these are linked so that if we can't control one, it often means we have no power whatever to control the others — job opportunities and finances, for example.

The opposite of powerlessness is, obviously, power. Power is defined in the dictionary as "the ability to act. Strength of force. The right, ability, or capacity to exercise control. Any form of energy that can perform work. Great or telling force or effect." Do we want power? Of course we do. For power is nothing more than using energy to effect a change for the better, and we certainly want to make life better than it has been. So how do we go about getting rid of powerlessness and gaining the power we want? For many alcoholics the first step was joining A.A. For the overeater it may have been O.A. In the same way, there are problems we may have outside of alcoholism or overeating, and there *are* ways to gain power over them.

In examining your list, suppose you had written the simple item, "Can't stop the rain." Think about it for a minute. What *can* you do in case of rain? It's almost a silly question. The first and most obvious answer is to come in *out* of the rain. Or, get an umbrella and slosh through the rain to your destination. Put your house plants out for a good soaking. Sing and dance in the rain. With a little imagination and willingness to have fun, you can probably come up with more ideas; some of them outlandish, some of them very useful. The main point here is that you do have not just one, but *many,* alternative ways of exercising power, acting — having an *effect* — in spite of the fact that you were "powerless" to stop the rain. As you can see, the first step away from powerlessness and toward power is to *think* and be willing to look at new solutions to a problem.

But let's consider a more realistic problem. Let's say that, for whatever reason, you quit high school and never got a high school diploma. Now you realize you're in a low-paying, dead-end job; you'll never get ahead, you'll never have nice things, and you feel powerless to do anything about it. The first step is to think. (Do this now, whether you're sitting by yourself with paper and pencil, or in a group.) After a few minutes, you should have some sort of list of actions that you *could* take. Select one or two that look most positive, and draw up a plan, step-by-step, for improving your life. Perhaps you've decided that taking a three-week typing course will help you get a better job. Do you work days? You can go to school at night or on the weekends. Do you work on changing shifts? Try talking about the problem with your boss and see if you can stay on one shift for the few weeks it would take to finish the course. Do you find that working and taking care of housework makes you too tired to take on school courses? Then drop the housework a while; it'll keep.

Preparing For Action

After considering your choices, it's time to prepare. This is extremely important in getting rid of powerlessness and gaining power. The word "power" carries with it a feeling of energy and vitality. Unfortunately, women have a tendency to keep on working no matter how tired they are, to keep giving, to keep on trying — long after they're exhausted and have no vitality or power left. So, in this preparation stage, it's important to ask yourself, "When was the last time I had a good night's sleep?" It's a simple question, and one women often easily overlook. You can't feel powerful when you're wiped out with fatigue. A person who is tired and keeps working often becomes depressed and, just as often, can't figure out why she is depressed, is making mistakes, and is unable to make things turn out right. A good night's sleep can have a very positive effect on your emotional well-being and on your skills too.

After you've thought through a problem, looked at possible ways to overcome it, and prepared yourself for achieving power over it, the final step can be the most difficult. The final step is to *act*. It may seem difficult to actually *do* something about your life simply because it's something you've never tried before. Doing anything new can be frightening because you're taking a risk. The baby learning to walk falls a lot. But if you've ever watched one, you realize he certainly doesn't stand up with the intention of walking across the room and out the door. He learns in little bits and pieces as skill and confidence grow. First, the baby will simply stand, holding onto a coffee table or a chair. Gradually, over days and weeks, the first step becomes two or three or four steps that grow into a tour around the table. A reach from the safety of the table becomes a quick, two-step lunge for another piece of furniture. It's a comical and joyful thing to watch a child walk many steps to mother's arms, and see him gaily *crawl* back to the starting point, stand up, and walk unaided to Mom again. Practicing over and over again, going a little farther each time, the child gains power over his own little legs and, sometimes to Mother's chagrin, his own little world. It's action, doing, power, that indicate growth and development. From that growth and development come real pleasure and happiness in life.

"We admitted we were powerless . . . ." A person who is curled up in a cocoon of powerlessness is really not much use to herself or to anyone else. Certainly she feels no joy in the possibilities available to her. But one who is willing to think, prepare, and act — to gain power — is one who, in spite of powerlessness over alcohol and other drugs, food, or other circumstances in life, will go on to lead a full and challenging life, full of risks perhaps, but also full of rewards and joys. "We *were* powerless . . . ," but think of what we can be!

SUCCESS AND FAILURE

Success is so often spelled with dollar signs — $ucce$$ — that it may be difficult for many women to relate to it. The homemaker tastes that dollar-sign success only through the accomplishments of her husband. The working woman who doesn't get paid as much as her male counterpart may be cheated of success. As she watches him climb the career ladder only to have a heart attack at an early age, she may wonder if this success is really what she wants.

In simple terms, success is the achievement of a particular goal; it's *any* accomplishment. But we tend to get it mixed up with our culture's special definition of success, which is really only one type of goal: that of job level and salary range. Men have judged themselves and each other by how much money they have earned and how much power they have in the companies they've worked for. Until recently, women weren't even considered candidates for this kind of success because most of us were at home, or were ignored because we earned such low pay. Women could stay at home, clean house, raise children, and never give a thought to success. That was something for a man to worry about.

But women are "in the world" now, many are striving for success, yet questioning what it is and whether we really want it. It's been said that women have a "fear of success" when we seem to hold back from doing the things men have done successfully. Perhaps this fear of success is really a sign that not all women have the same goals men do. $ucce$$ is not necessarily "success."

Defining Success

Faced with a great number of choices today, we must define success for ourselves. Success may mean achieving goals that are meaningful; if it's the dollar success of the once all-male business world, fine, but it should be *our* goal, not one that's been imposed on us by society. In an attempt to gain rightful equality with men, many women have run headlong toward the male success ladder without fully considering the consequences. Success, yes, but on whose terms?

If we're going to think about success and what it means, we also have to think about failure. It's *not* achieving a goal we set out to reach. Sometimes failure is not the result of something we did. A mother might devote her life to the well-being of her children, wishing happy, successful lives for them. If one of her children grows up to be a high school dropout or a drug addict, can she say she has failed as a mother? Not necessarily. No matter how good a mother she's been, she has no control over what kind of person her grown child will be. The woman who must quit school because she's widowed and has to support her family is no failure. The person who loses her job because of company layoffs is no failure, though she may feel like one for a time.

Success or failure in recovery is one instance where we *can* choose our own direction or choose to take some responsibility for our lives. Like anything else, however, our goals must be realistic. We may not be able to control what happens for the rest of our lives, but we can set goals for one day at a time: *today I will not drink; today I will stay on a diet; today I will be patient with myself and those around me.*

Setting Goals

Success and failure are issues women think about today, whether it's success in achieving personal goals or career goals, or success in recovery. We need to understand the ingredients that go into success.

First, you must define a reachable goal. Reachable, that is, for *you*. For instance, you're not likely to become a famous writer if you never finished high school and don't know how to read or write. You have to back up a bit and set a more reasonable goal of, perhaps, earning your equivalency diploma. If, however, you've had a good deal of training, the famous-writer goal may be attainable. The goal should be something *you* really want, not something you think you *should* do, or other people want you to do. Success is not worth the sacrifices you have to make to become a high-level banker when you hate banking! Once you define your goal, brainstorm the steps you have to take and how to put them into action. Then think about possible problems and barriers and how you might overcome them. In other words, be prepared. Be prepared, too, for the possibility of failure. What alternative goals can you set if circumstances beyond your control keep you from achieving success in one area? Successful people are willing to try again, find a new path, or set new goals.

Discuss success and failure with your group or with a friend. Share what success means to you and how it may differ for women and men. By setting realistic and meaningful goals you can enjoy true success in every aspect of your recovery.

SELF-IMAGE AND SELF-ESTEEM

Have you ever said, "I could never do that; it's just not me"? Have you ever admired someone who seemed to be able to do everything well? More often than not the difference between you and that other "achiever" is not ability, talent, or training, but self-image.

Self-image is our idea of who and what we are. It's the way we think of ourselves: a picture of our personality, appearance, sex appeal, what we can do. It's a reflection of how we think other people see us, too. Sometimes the image is clear and true and sometimes, like our reflections in the mirrors at the carnival, self-image is very distorted.

Closely linked with self-image is self-esteem, or self-respect. Self-esteem is an essential ingredient of good emotional mental health. Yet, women so often fail to give credit where credit is due — to ourselves — for our contributions to our families and to society. We take for granted, and everyone around us takes for granted, so many of our activities: the culinary skills for which a male chef receives awards, the office management skills that win promotions for bosses, the creative ability that produces beautiful needlework and other artwork, the intelligence that solves a husband's business problem during a talk at home, the community work done for free. Women achieve so much that goes unrecognized, unappreciated, and taken for granted, that it's no wonder we often have low self-esteem.

Self-respect
If we don't have respect for ourselves, we may end up being taken advantage of; if we don't have respect for ourselves, it's easy to let go of moral standards like honesty, kindness, caring, justice, mercy, dignity. A person with no self-respect will not respect others, will cheat on that exam, short-change that customer, etc. Self-respect is a form of love, and it's well known that if you don't love yourself, you can't truly love someone else. Like love, or the lack of it, esteem is passed on to others in a way that profoundly affects many lives — the lives of our spouses, our children, neighbors, and friends.

Esteem is recognition of accomplishments. It's praise we *deserve* for something we've done. Unfortunately, we have allowed society and our families to take us for granted. Our lack of self-esteem is reflected in statements we often hear like, "I'm just a housewife," "I'm just a secretary," or, "I'm just a nurse."

Self-image and self-esteem are first formed in childhood. Many of us developed a self-image of being lovable, capable, or desirable from messages and feedback we got from our parents, aunts and uncles, teachers, and friends. Unfortunately, some of us grew up believing we were ugly, not too bright, untalented, or undesirable. Like a self-fulfilling prophecy, we eventually *became* undesirable because we acted in ways that fit our beliefs. Self-image can work for us or against us. A woman who feels little respect for herself is going to have a very hard time achieving recovery. After all, why bother if you're not "worth" it? But a woman can make it in recovery if she knows she's worthy of self-esteem in spite of her problem with alcohol, other drugs, or overeating. Self-image and self-esteem rise and fall together. When one goes down, the other goes down. Let's take a look at some ways to improve both of them in ourselves.

Recognizing Our Worth
Where can we find recognition for our accomplishments in the home, on the job, or in the community? We must begin with ourselves. Here's an interesting exercise that may take you a

week or more to finish, but it's a real eye-opener. Make a list of 50 things you've accomplished in your life — 50 things you've learned or done well. Begin with things you've done recently. As you work at it, you'll find yourself jotting down forgotten memories, surprising yourself with activities from your childhood and adolescent years. A woman I know with a very poor self-image discovered that, as a teenager, she had talked a girl out of committing suicide. Not many of us can say that, yet it was something she'd completely forgotten through the years, losing sight of herself as a valuable human being. Remembering that wonderful achievement made a breakthrough in both her self-image and self-respect. So don't give up. Keep at it until you complete your list. Then share it with your group. Pat yourself on the back. You'll find that, in spite of past failures or problems that have given you a distorted self-image, self-esteem will come to you and open new pathways and motivation toward recovery. After all, you deserve it!

Self-image is first formed in childhood and *might* be negative. But, luckily, self-image *can* be changed. "When I was very young," said one middle-aged woman, "I had the idea I was a cold, not-too-friendly person. I mean, there were kids in school who *told* me I was cold, so that's pretty much the way I was. I felt shy and didn't have too many friends so I just sort of hung back. It wasn't until I was out of high school and working when all that changed. At work we were in constant contact with people, and we were expected to be friendly and helpful. People were friendly back. I learned how to be warm. The way I see myself has completely changed."

There are so many aspects to self-image it would be impossible to cover them all, but let's consider a few.

1. *Physical appearance:* are you pretty, sexy, glamorous, cute, petite, gangly, athletic, graceful, clumsy, plain?
2. *Personality:* are you friendly, cold, warm, outgoing, shy, bouncy, dignified, studious, scatterbrained, serious, jolly?
3. *Femininity:* are you feminine? This is an issue involving both appearance and personality that many women in

recovery have a problem with. This would be a good group topic to explore.
4. *Character:* are you honest, crafty, loyal, sneaky, kind?
5. *Capability:* are you creative, artistic, competent, inept, talented, disorganized?

What is *your* self-image? Is it a negative one that's going to be a stumbling block in recovery, or a positive one that will give you the push to keep striving for a better life? Make a self-image list: "I see myself as. . . ." Then go back and write down an example to back up each image point. For instance: "I see myself as a person who takes command of a situation" could be backed up with the behavior example, "When a problem comes up at work I make decisions and carry them out without having to check with my boss first." Another example: "I see myself as having no willpower at all." But the behavior notation might be, "That's not true because I *did* stay on my last diet for a long time; I almost reached my goal."

After you've gone over your list, share it with others and get their feedback. Put together the items which correctly size you up. Then go over your list again and decide which positive aspects you want to keep and which negative ones you want to change. This is a good time to set goals, brainstorm solutions to problem areas, and start practicing new behaviors. If you're indecisive, for example, don't start out by making big, life-changing decisions. Starting out with little ones will help build confidence. As your self-image changes for the better you'll find it easier to make the more complicated decisions. "Decisive" will replace "indecisive" on your self-image list!

Take a good look at yourself and your self-image. Does it agree with your list of 50 accomplishments? After all, if you could accomplish all those things, your self-image *must* be positive in many respects. If it's not, you may be playing a "false modesty" game. Go over your list again. Ask a close friend how she sees you; the difference may be surprising and may help you find out where your self-image is distorted. Then, *act* on it, practice the positive behaviors you've listed. If you change what you're doing, your self-image will change. You will come to like and have esteem for the most important person in your life — you. Recovery, the most important accomplishment of all, will surely follow.

PERSONAL RESPONSIBILITY

We are all responsible for carrying out certain duties in life, but sometimes we become overwhelmed and burned out when they are more than we can bear. Women have a tendency to take on responsibility for every big and little thing, partly out of habit and because we *care* so much about other people. But sometimes our sense of personal responsibility can be actually harmful to ourselves and others. How do we know where it begins and where it ends?

Let's decide first what it is. Let everyone in your group take turns defining what responsibility is.

Basically, responsibility has to do with being accountable for one's actions, or for being rightfully expected to do certain things. Let's question certain aspects of this idea.

If you look at your eating habits, for example, it's pretty obvious only you can be responsible for what and how much you eat. As an adult, you have the freedom and *capability* that a two-year-old child doesn't have. Because you are *capable* of selection, you are *responsible* for your diet. But suppose you're in the hospital with broken arms and legs. You surely can't trot down to the local fruit stand for your daily apple. Responsibility for your diet has shifted to the hospital staff. This example illustrates that it can only be carried out by the capable party. When ability is absent, responsibility (and authority) shifts.

Mothers are very responsible people. In fact, they get so accustomed to being totally responsible for their children that they often take responsibility for them as adults. When little Johnny becomes twelve or thirteen years old and still won't tie his own shoes, something is definitely wrong. Here's a case where personal responsibility should have shifted, but didn't. Even though Mother is still capable of tying Johnny's shoes, so is Johnny. This duty must shift if Johnny is to reach his potential as a human being, and if Mother is ever to get up off her knees.

Drawing The Lines

Sometimes women take on obligations not only because we are capable but because we *care*. We care about the environment, the Red Cross, the Humane Society, Jerry's Kids, public television, cancer research, Easter Seals, and so many other causes whose goals would never be realized without our help. With the best intentions we might decide to contribute to all of them, only to find out that, oops!, there's no grocery money left for the family. Caring has outstripped our capability and, though we may regret it, we must pick and choose and set priorities. Once again, responsibility is contingent on capability. In this example, we share the tasks with others.

It's quite possible that when you decided to fight your particular problem — whether it's alcohol, other drug abuse, overeating, or whatever — you were told you must take personal responsibility for your recovery and, of course, that's true. All the help and support of your family, friends, and counselors will come to nothing unless you accept personal responsibility for your own actions and emotional health. Only you can make it happen. But women so often tend to take on more than is feasible for good emotional health.

This is a good time to assess your roster of responsibilities. Have you taken on more than you can bear? Have you, like so many women, allowed others to load their burdens onto your shoulders? Are they interfering with your recovery?

As you grow and change, your responsibilities will shift and change. You will give up some, share others, and take on new ones. This will be true for your children, family members, spouse, friends, and co-workers, too. Remember that your responsibility begins with capability and ends when capability shifts or ends. Why not take stock of your responsibilities today?

GUILT

If you're in a group, or grappling with a problem alone, try having a session on *guilt*. Think of all the ways you are currently using the word *guilt* to describe how you feel or how you are reacting to a problem. Take your time. You might want to jot down some of the examples your group members share.
Now let's discuss what is this thing called *guilt*. It's a word that is battered and bruised from overuse and misuse. Women seem to be particularly susceptible to feelings that are labeled guilt, and it doesn't matter whether they are in recovery from drug abuse or have led pristine lives. It's a word used to label certain feelings and it needs some close examination. Let's look at some examples here and see how many you can come up with yourself or in your group.
An obese person might say, "I had a piece of Boston cream pie last night and I feel so guilty about it."
A parent says, "I found out my babysitter had stolen some money from my purse, and when I confronted her I felt guilty about it."
A divorced mother confides, "I have to go to work if I'm to feed the kids, but I feel so guilty about it."
A young wife says, "I went to a Tupperware party up the block while my husband babysat. I didn't get home until midnight and I felt so guilty."
The foreman of the jury says, "We find the defendant guilty of murder in the first degree."
These are five uses of the word guilty and only one of them is correct. Take a look at the five examples above (along with those you thought of yourself), and you might see a common thread in four of them.
Did you find it? It's the word *feel*. In the first four examples here, each person said, "I feel" or "I felt guilty." And that's where we run into trouble with this misused and overused word. Guilt is not an emotion. It is a verdict. If we drag out the dictionary, we see that guilt means the fact of having committed

a breach of conduct, as in violating a law, committing a crime. This is the strictly correct meaning of guilt. Guilt implies blame for doing something wrong. Often when we don't even realize it fully, we are actually blaming ourselves for wrongdoing when we may have done nothing wrong at all.
It's a lot like using the word *bad*. "I feel bad." What does that mean? "I feel sick to my stomach." "I feel evil." "I feel sad." "I feel tired." "I feel remorse for hurting someone's feelings." "I'm in pain because I just got out of surgery." When you compare an overused word like bad to the overused word guilt you can get an idea why confusion results.

Expressing Our Feelings
We are what we say we are. Women are particularly susceptible to the misuse of the word guilt. Think about conversations you've had with your women friends or in your women's therapy group. Let's say your friend is the divorced mother who says, "I have to go to work to feed the kids but I feel so guilty about it. . . ." Her voice trails off into silence, and even over the telephone you can sense her depression and tension. There's a sense, too, of inaction. She's trapped with this "feeling" of guilt and is paralyzed, unable to act on it.

If you take the word guilty and substitute bad, right away you may ask, "What do you really mean by that?" Ask your friend, or yourself if you're the one in this predicament, "What does it really mean?" As we've done before, let's brainstorm some possibilities. "I have to go to work and I feel very anxious about the safety of the children while I'm away." Or, "I have to go to work and I feel regret because I'm too tired when I get home to give them the loving attention I used to." "I have to go to work and I feel angry because I'm carrying the responsibilities of two people." "I have to go to work and I feel a sense of loss because I don't have the time to do nice things for the children, like bake cookies for the fun of it, or sit down with them for a game, or have the patience to listen to things they want to tell me."

Now we're getting someplace. That one misused word, guilt, was covering up your true feelings of anxiety, worry, regret, loss, anger, or resentment. And because that one word was used to cover up all those true feelings, it also killed any real chance of defining the problem and doing something to solve it. You can't do anything about guilt. If you committed a crime, you're guilty and that's that. But you can do something about feelings and problems associated with worry, anger, etc. For example, if the divorced mother realizes it's not guilt she feels but worry about the safety of her children, she has several options open to her to remove that worry. She can think through her particular situation and look for ways to solve the problem. If one of her children is a teenager, she can have a serious talk with him about her concerns, and give him responsibility for the younger ones after school. If all her children are young, she can hire a babysitter or make arrangements with a neighbor, or a childcare center. This is not to make light of the problem; solutions are not always easy to find. But where guilt leaves no room for action, concern and worry are signals that action can (and probably must), be taken in some form.

Guilt feelings are often expressed by alcoholic women who are mothers. Many an alcoholic mother has said, "I feel so guilty about what my drinking has done to my children." Again we must ask, "What, exactly, does she mean by that?" Does she mean, "I am guilty of abusing alcohol (that makes sense and is correct), and as a result I feel a sense of regret because I have lost my children's trust"? This makes sense, it may be correct, and it's something you can work to change.

Hopefully we can see that using the word guilt indiscriminately has a tendency to cover up the identity of a problem and, as a result, covers up any possibility of a solution to the problem. We can also see that changing the word guilt to bad and then getting to the bottom of what's really bothering us can lead to action for improving our situation.

What is this grand affair we seem to have with guilt? I think women, either by nature or by training, tend to be more emotional than men. Our emotions are closer to the surface, more readily laid bare, right out there for ourselves and the world to see. And what have we been doing all these years? Misusing and abusing that word, guilt — like the word bad — as though it could explain that incredible range of emotions we experience. We can't blame only ourselves for this misuse. Professionals in psychiatry, psychology, counselors in social work, authors of books — all of them — have applied the word guilt where it simply does not belong; and that use has filtered down to the rest of us. Using that word has clouded the real issues of our feelings, and in many cases has prevented us from action for improvement.

Is there ever a time when guilt is good? Yes, absolutely — *if* we remember what it really means. Guilt is not a feeling. It is a statement of a fact. A person who is habitually unkind to those around him, yet refuses to acknowledge that he is unkind — and does not admit to his guilt in the matter — is not ever going to change for the good. "I didn't do anything" is the usual denial of such a person. An obese person who cries, "I can't help it that I'm fat; my mother overfed me" is a person who has denied his or her guilt for *remaining* obese by overeating. In these and so many other cases, acknowledgment of guilt where guilt actually exists is the essential first step toward recovery. If you acknowledge that you're the one who's guilty, then you are the one with the power to change.

SHAME

We've talked about guilt and the idea that it's not an emotion as we often believe, but a statement of fact about our actions. Shame, however, *is* a painful emotion that results from guilt. It comes from the realization that we are guilty of demeaning acts. These acts make us appear to be something less than we are or something less than other people. We may blush with shame, or feel a tightness in the pit of the stomach. We may feel we can't look another person straight in the eye, or cringe at the thought that others look down on us. Shame is the opposite of pride. Shame is a difficult emotion to live with.

Facing Our Shame

As difficult as it is to face our shame, this is often the first step taken on the road to recovery. Looking at shame can be a guide to emotional health, if we refuse to allow it to control our lives. Let's take a closer look at this emotion.

We often hear people say, "That person is really rotten; he has no shame for the things he's done." Murder, for instance, is a terrible crime, yet we feel a double sense of horror if the murderer feels no remorse. What about slumlords who take their tenants' rent, yet feel no shame that those tenants are living in squalor, without heat or water? We look down on them for their lack of shame. We may feel the same about those who engage in pornography, or who are cruel to others. It's obvious to us that if they feel no sense of shame, there is something wrong with them. Something is out of kilter.

A person who abuses alcohol or other drugs, without a thought, is a person destroying herself and those around her. But when she wakes up to a sense of shame, it's a clear signal her conscience is alive and well. In this case, shame may be the driving force that makes her seek help. Shame says, "I care, and I've got to change things for the better." This is the healthy aspect of this painful emotion.

Although none of us likes to feel it, we can use shame to guide our future actions. To use a fairly simple example, if you're an overeater and you're reaching for the refrigerator door, don't eat first and feel ashamed later. Stop for a moment, imagine yourself taking that forbidden food, allow yourself to feel *now* the sense of shame you would feel later, and decide whether you want to live with your self-reproach and failure. Very often getting in touch with this emotion can tell you the right thing to do.

Of course, too much of any thing can be harmful. And so it is with this painful emotion. *Don't wallow in shame.* Let it be your guide but not your warden. If you are so bound up with shame that you're afraid to move, then you must overcome it. Identify it, brainstorm it, attack it with possible solutions or ways to make up for whatever you did. And then, let go of it. Let go and let God.

Think about your own sense of shame. Do you lack shame even though you are guilty of real wrongdoing? Or are you so deeply immersed in it that it prevents you from reaching out to others with love? Then let go of it. Are you so deeply ashamed of your drinking that you want to reach for more to forget? Then let go of it. Turn your back on it if you must. It has served its purpose and served you well, or you would not have sought treatment. Walk away from it now, and walk in peace.

CHOICES

Years ago and in ages past, people didn't have very many choices open to them. A child born to a serf in the Middle Ages would grow up to be a serf himself. Although society did change through the centuries so that a person could better himself, in general, a son followed in his father's footsteps and became whatever his father had been. The farmer's son became a farmer; the coalminer's son worked in the mines. The craftsman's son learned his father's craft, or might be apprenticed to another, but the choice was seldom his to make. Time, education, and society changed all that, and recent generations of men found new freedom in the choices they could make for becoming the kind of men they wanted to be. Women, of course, were a different story. With few exceptions, women were expected to fit the "kitchen, church, and children" mold as dutiful wives and mothers. Servant's wife, merchant's wife, or wife of a duke, it was all the same. Their fathers made life decisions for them until their husbands took rule and, for many, later life found them depending on their sons for guidance.

Today, women's freedom to make choices is almost overwhelming. In fact, women may have more choices to make than men! After all, men are still expected to be the breadwinners in the family, but women can now have business careers if they want to, or they can opt to stay home and have babies, too. Nor can we forget the four million single mothers in this country who must make choices that deeply affect not only their own lives, but the lives and well-being of their children. Let's take a look at some of the choices women not only *can,* but in some cases *must* make, today.

Today one can choose to marry or not to marry, have children or not, select a career, go to college while caring for children, remain married, or divorce (a choice virtually unheard of only thirty years ago). These are only a few of the big, long-range choices women can make today. Then you have other choices: whether to drink or not drink (if you're not alcoholic), stay on your diet or give it up, even whether to read a particular kind of book, or see a movie that may affect your outlook on life. (Remember, only a few decades ago women were not even allowed to vote.)

Choosing Our Paths

Making a choice is making a decision to follow one particular path while leaving another. It's saying yes to one line of action and no to others. Sometimes the pressure to make a decision can seem overwhelming. Nobody wants to make a mistake that will adversely affect her life. Sometimes it happens that the possibilities are so confusing we wind up putting off a firm decision. We drift along, afraid to lose what we do have, yet not gaining that better situation.

Let's look at some decision-making techniques that are easy, practical ways of selecting a course of action. All they require is paper and pencil, along with a willingness to think and to get in touch with your feelings. For our example, let's use a problem many women are facing today: whether or not to return to work.

At the top of the page, write down the problem/choice: to return to work or stay home. This may seem silly because you've been grappling with the problem in your mind for weeks and you think you certainly ought to know what the problem is by now. Well, maybe not. When a problem runs through your head, it tends to run in twenty different directions, creating confusion. But writing it down makes it clear, holds it in place so you can look at it and see it for what it really is. Perhaps you'll look at this problem and think, What am I saying? To work or not to work? I'm divorced, can barely feed my kids on the support I'm getting and my rent is going up next month. I *have* to go to work; there is no choice. But my children are so young I don't want to be away from them for long. The problem to be defined then becomes something entirely different. Now you can write it down as: "to work full-time or to work part-time." You now have a specific decision to make and can go on to the next step.

Draw a line down the center of the page to make two columns. Let one column be for the part-time and the other for full-time work. In each column, write down all the advantages you can think of for each one, all the good points. You'll probably be able to see very quickly that one type of job has more advantages for you than the other.

Now you can take another page with two columns and write down all the disadvantages to each type of job. Again, you'll be able to see that one column is more filled up than the other, and the best choice is so much easier to make.

But what if the columns look fairly equal? What if the list of advantages, for instance, looks about the same for both types of work? If this is the case, you can use a little trick of the decision-making technique. Go back over the lists, and on a scale of one to ten, write down next to each item a number that measures how important that item is to you. Now's the time to get in touch with your feelings. For example, if your children are very young and it's extremely important to you to spend a lot of time with them, you might have listed under advantages to part-time work: "More time with the children." Let's say you feel strongly about that, so you give it a ten. On the other hand, if your children are a bit older and don't really need you every minute they're home from school (they might be away from home with after-school jobs), you might give that item only a four or five. Using the numbers system is a useful way of discovering how you really feel about different advantages and disadvantages of the choices you can make. When you add up all the numbers, it's often surprising how easy it is to make the final choice. Basically, this is just a different form of brainstorming.

Let's take this one step further. Suppose you've arrived at what looks like the best possible choice. You've made a decision and you think it's the right one, but you're a little bit skeptical about a few of its disadvantages. Well, now's the time to look at ways of making compromises to achieve your goals. You might take a better-paying job farther from home because you do need the money, but make a point of setting aside special weekend time for your children that you normally would have spent on other activities. It's a trade-off. It may not be perfect, but it will help you achieve your most important goal, or solve the problem that was plaguing you.

A final word about choices. Somehow most of us have the idea that when we make a choice or a decision, it's chiseled in stone and we're going to be stuck with it for the rest of our lives. This is often the very reason we are fearful of making choices in the first place. Is a decision chiseled in stone? Of course not. If we can learn to make one decision, we can make ten decisions. We can evaluate new situations and change our minds. We can change our jobs, quit school, move on to new challenges, or go back to where we were before. We can make decisions now, and all the choices are ours.

RELATIONSHIPS

Everyone knows that when a beautiful, delicious-smelling meal is placed in front of you, you begin to salivate. In fact, if you're hungry enough, just thinking about a favorite food will make your mouth water. To psychologists who study behavior, the food or the thought of food is called a stimulus, and salivating is called a response. People and animals both respond to the sensations around them. If a blast of cold air hits us, we shiver. If we whistle to a trained dog, it will come to us.

Imagine yourself walking down your street on the way to the grocery store. The sun is shining, the air is clear, and you feel good. A neighbor of yours is walking toward you, and as you pass her by you smile and say, "Hi." She ignores you, turns her head away, and just walks by. Suddenly you're surprised and then downright annoyed. Suddenly you don't feel good. This is how people can affect each other, and is an example of stimulus-response behavior. Your neighbor's behavior was the stimulus, and your annoyance was the response.

Here's another example. You're walking down the street (again . . . you're a busy woman), and you're preoccupied with how you're going to pay the phone bill and the electricity bill on time this month. A friend you haven't seen in a while appears and cheerfully says "Hi" and hugs you. Suddenly you feel happy and flushed with pleasure. The stimulus was your friend's cheerfulness and hug; the response was your feeling of pleasure. Again, it's apparent that people can strongly affect each other's feelings and reactions. One person acts; the other reacts. Sometimes we spend our whole lives responding to others without realizing we're doing it. And we may spend our whole lives affecting other people in ways we would never guess. The stimulus-response pattern of behavior is, in many respects, a difficult one to break. Yet, if we're to take control of our lives and make them worth living, we need to understand how to make our relationships more than just responses.

Let's look at a typical problem suffered by the wife of a male alcoholic. Let's say he hasn't been drinking for several weeks. For a change, things are relatively peaceful at home, but he's quiet and moody most of the time and she and the children sort of tiptoe around him. Although the house is peaceful, the people in it are tense and subdued. They are responding to the alcoholic's "dry drunk." You can see the importance here of breaking out of the stimulus-response style of living. Indeed, one of the first things a member of Al-Anon must learn is to stop reacting to the alcoholic and go out and start making her own life livable.

Breaking Habits

Although we are built, like all creatures, to respond to stimuli, we humans are blessed with brains that can actually interfere with the stimulus-response pattern. In fact, most of our brainpower is devoted to *stopping* actions, not starting them. So how do you go about breaking out of the stimulus-response pattern of living? The simplest step is to make yourself aware of how you react to other people, and take a moment to think about the stimulus and what might have been your habitual response. For example, your child comes bursting into the house after school, mad as a hornet, slams his books down, and charges off to his room in a huff. Your reflex reaction might be to charge in after him and demand an explanation for coming into the house like that. His stimulus of anger would result in your response of anger. But if you pause for a moment and take a deep breath, you say, "Hmm. Something must have upset him pretty badly. Let me stay calm and see if the gentle approach would help." Taking control of such simple, momentary reactions can go a long way toward making your relationships better. But it's even more important to take stock of how you may have built up a habitual way of behaving toward another person, not just in moments, but all the time, because of his or her personality. Your response has become a *pattern* of behaving toward another's personality.

I know a woman who has several children and she's always marvelled at how they differ from one another. "Two of my children are openly affectionate and think nothing of coming to me for a hug for no particular reason. When I think back on it, I could kick myself for not realizing that one child — who's always tended to be shy about showing his feelings — was *dying* to get that hug or kiss goodnight. Of course, when he was little I showed him affection, but for a long time as he was growing up, I just assumed he didn't want or need it if he didn't ask for it. Eventually, I reacted by not giving it. But I guess it bothered me, and when it dawned on me that I had to make the first move, I was amazed that he practically jumped at the chance the first time I said, 'Come, give me a kiss goodnight and go to bed.' He was about twelve years old then. Now he's fifteen and from time to time I still have to make that first move, but he lights up when I do, and he has learned to make the first move himself. We're so much closer now with this give-and-take."

This situation is no different than that of the spouse who tends to be afraid of making the first move when giving affection or sharing feelings, or that person you sit close to at the office who hardly ever says a word, or that woman who strikes you as someone you'd like to have as a friend. Instead of responding to his or her aloofness by being distant yourself, you can take a risk and be the one who reaches out with a friendly gesture of affection. I think we all share a basic fear of rejection, or sometimes we feel embarrassed to show our own positive feelings for someone else. But if we practice taking small risks by extending ourselves toward others instead of merely reacting to them, eventually we'll find reaching out for another is as natural as sun and rain. We'll be the ones providing positive stimuli, and they'll respond to our warmth.

Positive Action

Let's brainstorm this business of stimulus-response (s-r) relationships. You can do this alone or with your group. Think of the people with whom you have developed S-R relations. A son. A daughter. In-laws. Your spouse. Your boss. How is the S-R habit affecting your relationships with them? Think, too, of ways in which you might be providing a negative stimulus toward someone else. Are you the shy one who waits for others to say hello first? Do you tend to frown a lot? Are you, perhaps, one of those who doesn't trust other women? If you are, you will definitely be sending out signals (stimuli) of posture, facial expression, and tone of voice that will let other women know you don't trust them. They will respond by distrusting you! By responding to stimuli rather than thinking about what they really mean, we set up stereotypes of other people that block our ability to reach out to them. Perhaps the black person sees a white face and responds to it with resentment. Perhaps the obese person sees a slim one and responds with envy, which is a form of hatred. You look at your boss and see an authority figure instead of a person. Things can get bad enough when we respond to stimuli without thinking. They're even worse if we respond to stimuli that are really stereotypes.

People responding to each other is what relationships are all about. If you're a recovering person, it's important to realize that while you were drinking or while you were experiencing the dry drunk or while you were filled with self-loathing because of your obesity, you were sending out stimuli that were not normal. Your family, therefore, did not respond to you in a normal way. Your relationships became disjointed and warped. Now you must think of ways of breaking out of the S-R habit.

Again, try brainstorming your relationships with others. Look at their stimuli and your responses, but also take a good, hard look at the stimuli you provide. Plan ways to change the negative stimuli or the negative responses. Look for ways to increase the pleasant stimuli and the positive responses. Changing your relationships with others takes time and effort, but there's nothing more worth the effort than caring enough to love another person and to learn they love you.

FAITH

When we face reality, it may seem difficult to have faith. To have faith is to believe in something we cannot see with our eyes or feel with our hands, to know with complete confidence that God exists or that there is a Power greater than ourselves we can rely on, or that certain values will never change. Each day we are reminded that somewhere in the world there is a war. Each day we work hard and struggle to achieve some decency in our lives — some semblance of comfort — and find it a losing battle. We had faith that our marriages would last and now many of us are divorced. We had faith that if we loved our children they would turn out to be happy, successful people and now we enter them in drug therapy programs. We had faith in the teachings of our religions and now, every day, some scientist discovers some new way to explain our existence without God.

"Faith" carries with it a connotation of belief in a god or a religion. But it is more than that. Faith also means any belief that is the foundation of an individual's hopes, goals, feelings, and behavior. It is a foundation or a guide for living. But with all the disappointments and disillusionment we've suffered we may well wonder if it is possible to have faith today. In a moment of despair it may be easy enough to say, no. We may feel we have lost our faith in many ways — lost something we thought was absolutely permanent.

This is a good moment to share with your recovery group all your ideas of what faith is (or, if necessary, what it was before you lost it). Have someone write down the various concepts of faith, and see if you can come up with some basic similarities in group members' definitions. Brainstorm your definitions of faith.

Now let's take a look at an article of faith so many of us once shared. We knew, with unshakeable faith, that on Christmas Eve Santa Claus would come, no matter what. We never saw him, but we believed, and on the basis of that belief we tiptoed around trying to be good, knowing he could see us and that he cared. As we grew up we learned the truth: he wasn't really there. Perhaps we suffered disappointment, disillusionment, maybe even a sense of betrayal. But what did we do? We went right on as adults and passed on that belief to our children, determined that they should have the joy of believing in the Santa Claus we once knew. In our growth and maturity, in our knowledge that Santa Claus is really ourselves, we have enjoyed the pleasure of faith in our own ability to love and give. We still believe, in some larger way, that Santa Claus exists. We make him exist within ourselves, and we could do that only when we matured enough to expand and grow, and look at our belief from a new point of view.

In sharing our definitions of faith, we may learn the form of our faith was supposed to be permanent. Somehow we've gotten the idea that, if we grew up believing God was a male spirit with a long gray beard and we can no longer believe in this image we have lost our faith in God. If we don't believe in that form, we don't believe at all. This isn't the case with everyone. There are millions of people who have gotten past their disillusionment with a narrow form of faith, and have expanded their concept of God to include the female spirit. They refer to God as She. Still others have found belief in an awesome "It" — a creative force that made the galaxies; a force they can wonder about and from which they can find an inspiration for living. It's heartening to realize that for those who are willing to grow and mature, to look at their beliefs with open minds, faith comes to them in a newer and more wonderful form than ever before.

Finding Inspiration

Of all the Twelve Steps, Step Two is sometimes the hardest. We think we've lost our faith when, in reality, we've only temporarily misplaced our ability to look at our faith in a new light. Do you believe earthquakes are bound to destroy life? Then you must also look at the other side and see that when the earth settles, people rebuild their homes and new flowers grow. If you see one side of a thing, you must also look at it from another side if you are going to truly understand it. So it is with faith. Faith in God. Faith in yourself. Faith in love and ideals. When you take the word "faith" and turn it into the word "belief" you can easily ask yourself, What do I believe in now? It's easy to discover you *do* have beliefs right now that enrich and shape your life.

An adult child of an alcoholic says, "If the world fell apart tomorrow and everything I ever believed in was destroyed, I would still know in my heart that my father loved me. Yes, there was a lot of pain from his drinking, but when I finally learned what alcoholism does to a person, I suddenly understood what had happened to him through the years was not his fault but what the drink had done to him. I knew then, with unshakeable faith, that he loved me and that the goodness and strength I have come from him. Knowing this, I've been able to face life's problems with a strength I never knew I had. He's been gone a long time, but I believe in his love and pride in me."

For another woman, the important things in life are love and knowledge. "I just can't see one without the other. I mean, you could have all the knowledge in the world but what good is it without love? On the other hand, as you grow by learning new things, it seems to me you just have so much to offer and bring to a loving relationship. If I had to choose money, power, fame, or anything else, I would go with knowledge and love. To me, they make life worth living."

You might believe in the value of Al-Anon, O.A., and the work of the Humane Society. Your beliefs might lie in the importance of the family, or in community service, or self-development. But whatever it may be, thinking you don't have faith in something is simply not realizing that your faith lies in what is most important to you right now.

Begin with what is important to you. It's the basis of a faith you may simply have not recognized. Write down "the things that are important to me." There is your faith; there are your beliefs. There is where we find a Power greater than ourselves, for these beliefs are the things that make us what we are. This, truly, is the foundation for everything we hope to be.

FULFILLMENT AND SELF-ACTUALIZATION

We have talked of success and know, somehow, that success and fulfillment are not quite the same thing. In the past fifteen or twenty years, "fulfillment" is something we women have been seeking to call our own as never before. Oddly enough, discussions of fulfillment seem to fill us with emptiness, a sense of longing, of grasping for something we're not sure exists even though we want it badly. We sense we have a right to it; somehow it is bound up with our American right to the "pursuit of happiness"; yet most discussions of fulfillment leave us dissatisfied. Mention fulfillment and many confusing questions arise.

The mother who was once content to be a homemaker now wishes she had a career. The single career woman pines for the marriage and children she never had. It's as though each one has discovered that certain aspects of their lives were neglected, and makes the mistake of thinking her life is now empty. In fact, their lives are at least half full. Each one has satisfied certain basic human needs. The homemaker has satisfied a basic human need to love, be loved, and to nurture. The career woman has satisfied a basic human need for using talents and gaining the respect of her peers. So, why are these women feeling unfulfilled?

Human beings have many needs because we have many capabilities. Let's look at needs like nutrition and vitamins. A person can enjoy what looks like a well-balanced diet. But if that diet is greatly lacking a single element like iodine, the seemingly healthy (fulfilled) person will develop a disfiguring goiter. The goiter could have been avoided if that basic need for iodine had been satisfied. Knowing your basic human needs can help prevent physical or emotional illness.

Let's take this nutrition example one step further to point out that, while everyone's needs are the same, there are differences in the *proportions* of our needs, and there are differences in the *timing* of our needs. Women, for instance, need more iron and calcium than men because their bodies use these chemicals differently. We all need these elements, but in different amounts. We know a newborn infant can grow and thrive solely on its mother's milk. But if an adult tried to live solely on milk, she would surely die of malnutrition, and might first even suffer ill effects from having ingested too much Vitamin D. Too much of something can be just as harmful as too little.

Identifying Needs

We can clear up some of the confusion about fulfillment by applying these examples. Let's say fulfillment is the satisfaction of all our basic human needs, just as good health comes from the satisfaction of all our basic nutritional needs. What are those needs? As you grow in recovery, you'll probably hear or read about a lot of different theories of what creates emotional and psychological health. But there is no perfect answer. I'd like to offer a theory that has made sense to me through the years because it's hopeful and very practical.

Unlike most psychiatrists who study emotional disorders, Abraham Maslow spent the better part of his life studying people who seemed to enjoy unusually good psychological health. They were a cut above the crowd. They were fulfilled human beings. They were what he called *self-actualizers*. Although they came from many different walks of life, they all enjoyed the satisfaction of certain needs that Maslow decided must be essential for human beings. He rated those needs on a scale from low to high, and discovered if the lower needs were not satisfied, it was difficult for a person to satisfy the higher ones. They would thus be prevented from becoming fulfilled, self-actualized people.

The needs are as follows:

1) physical needs: food, shelter, protective clothing, etc.

2) safety needs: security, freedom from fear, stability, and orderliness.

3) belonging needs and love needs: family relationships, friends, peer relations, neighborhood relations, affection.

4) esteem needs: self-respect and the deserved respect of others through competence or achievement, recognition, appreciation.

5) self-actualization needs: doing or being what the individual is fitted for, realizing the potential of one's own nature.

Using the needs scale, let's go all the way back to the beginning and examine the lives of the unfulfilled homemaker and the unfulfilled career woman. The unfulfilled homemaker says, "I have a nice home, no money problems, a lovely family, a good husband, and still I feel discontent. What's wrong with me?" Obviously, this woman's physical, safety, and love needs have been satisfied. Discontent is not a sign that something is wrong, but a sign that everything is right *on this level* of her needs as a human being. She is ready, at this point in her life, to go on to a higher level of personal development. This woman might ask herself whether her esteem needs are being satisfied in her role as a homemaker. If they are, then it's quite possible she should look higher on the scale. Perhaps her children are in school or even leaving home as they reach adulthood. Now she can think of someone she may not have paid much attention to for a long time — herself. Many women have discovered the joy of going back to school, to college, not with a future career in mind, but just for the happy discovery that their brain cells are alive and that it's *fun* to learn. Some find their fun in the rigors of the laboratory, others in front of an artist's easel where they can pour out their creative talents. Each one gets in touch with her *own* personality and interests, and feels fulfilled.

What about the career woman who feels unfulfilled? If she checks the needs scale, it may be obvious the career that satisfied her physical needs, her belonging, and esteem needs has actually undermined her safety needs. What safety needs? If she's been successful and doesn't have to worry about where her next meal is coming from, or the roof over her head, perhaps she's reached a position that requires her to make business trips at a moment's notice, trips that find her in strange cities or away from friends during traditional holidays, away from her home base and sense of stability and orderliness to her life. Perhaps that's what she needs to correct in order to restore a sense of balance and fulfillment to her life. But as another possibility, perhaps the scale shows her love needs have gone by the wayside. Does this mean that at the age of 45 or 50 she has to start looking for a husband and risk having a baby of her own? No. She can also look at the possibility of doing volunteer work in her spare time — not as a charity committee member but in a hands-on situation, working with children in a recreation center, or with the aged who are alone.

If you're feeling discontented and unfulfilled at this point in your life, use the needs scale as a guide to pinpointing where the problem exists. Identify the problem, brainstorm possible solutions, set a goal, make a plan to achieve it, and *act* on it.

Remember your needs will change, grow, and develop at different stages of your life, and your needs may be slightly different from those of your neighbor or friend. Remember, too, discontent and dissatisfaction are positive signs you are ready for new growth and new levels of fulfillment. Is fulfillment something you attain and that's the end of it? No. The little first-grader in school may learn to read and may enjoy the fulfillment of being able to read nursery rhymes and fairy tales. But as she grows, that level of fulfillment will not be enough. She wants a higher level of reading, seeks it out, and with that striving gains even greater satisfaction. And that's the often unrecognized pleasure the quest for fulfillment gives. No matter how far you've come, there is always the tickle of knowing things can get even better. Use the needs scale as a guide for setting the goals that lead to fulfillment in your life. It can assist you as you journey in recovery from obesity, alcoholism, emotional illness, or drug abuse. For what *is* recovery if not the achievement of the fullest self you can be?

The Twelve Steps of A.A.

1. We admitted we were powerless over alcohol — that our lives had become unmanageable.
2. Came to believe that a Power greater than ourselves could restore us to sanity.
3. Made a decision to turn our will and our lives over to the care of God *as we understood Him.*
4. Made a searching and fearless moral inventory of ourselves.
5. Admitted to God, to ourselves, and to another human being the exact nature of our wrongs.
6. Were entirely ready to have God remove all these defects of character.
7. Humbly asked Him to remove our shortcomings.
8. Made a list of all persons we had harmed, and became willing to make amends to them all.
9. Made direct amends to such people wherever possible, except when to do so would injure them or others.
10. Continued to take personal inventory and when we were wrong promptly admitted it.
11. Sought through prayer and meditation to improve our conscious contact with God *as we understood Him,* praying only for knowledge of His will for us and the power to carry that out.
12. Having had a spiritual awakening as the result of these Steps, we tried to carry this message to alcoholics, and to practice these principles in all our affairs.

---

*The Twelve Steps reprinted with permission of A.A. World Services, Inc.